Retro Groovy Cats
Coloring Book for Grown-Ups
Volume 1
by Karen Douglas

Retro Groovy Cats Coloring Book for Grown-ups, Volume 1
Copyright ©2016 Karen Douglas

All rights reserved. This book or any portion thereof
may not be reproduced or used in any manner whatsoever
without the express written permission of the publisher
except for the use of brief quotations in a book review.

Printed in the United States of America

First Printing, 2016   ISBN-13: 978-0692682067, ISBN-10: 0692682066

Retro Coloring Books
P.O. Box 725
Oak Grove, MO 64075

www.retrocoloringbooks.com

A quick sampling of pages

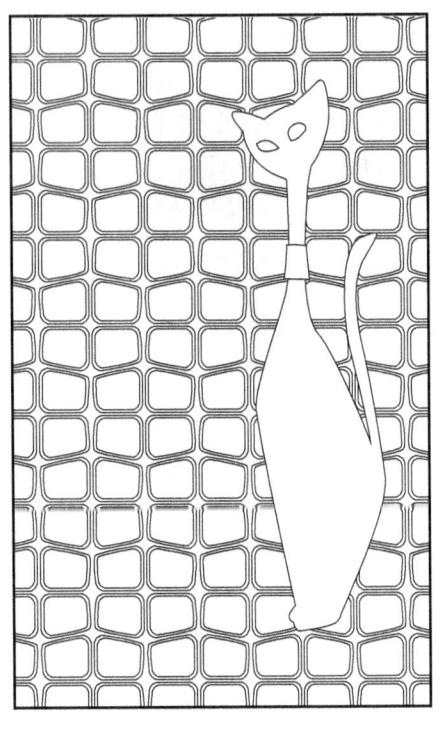

The pages of this book are suitable for colored pencils, markers and a variety of other media. To help prevent bleed-through, you may want to place a blank sheet of paper between the pages when coloring.

Each of the pages are intentionally left blank on the back side so that you don't have to worry about bleed-thru ruining the next image and to make it more convenient for removal and display.

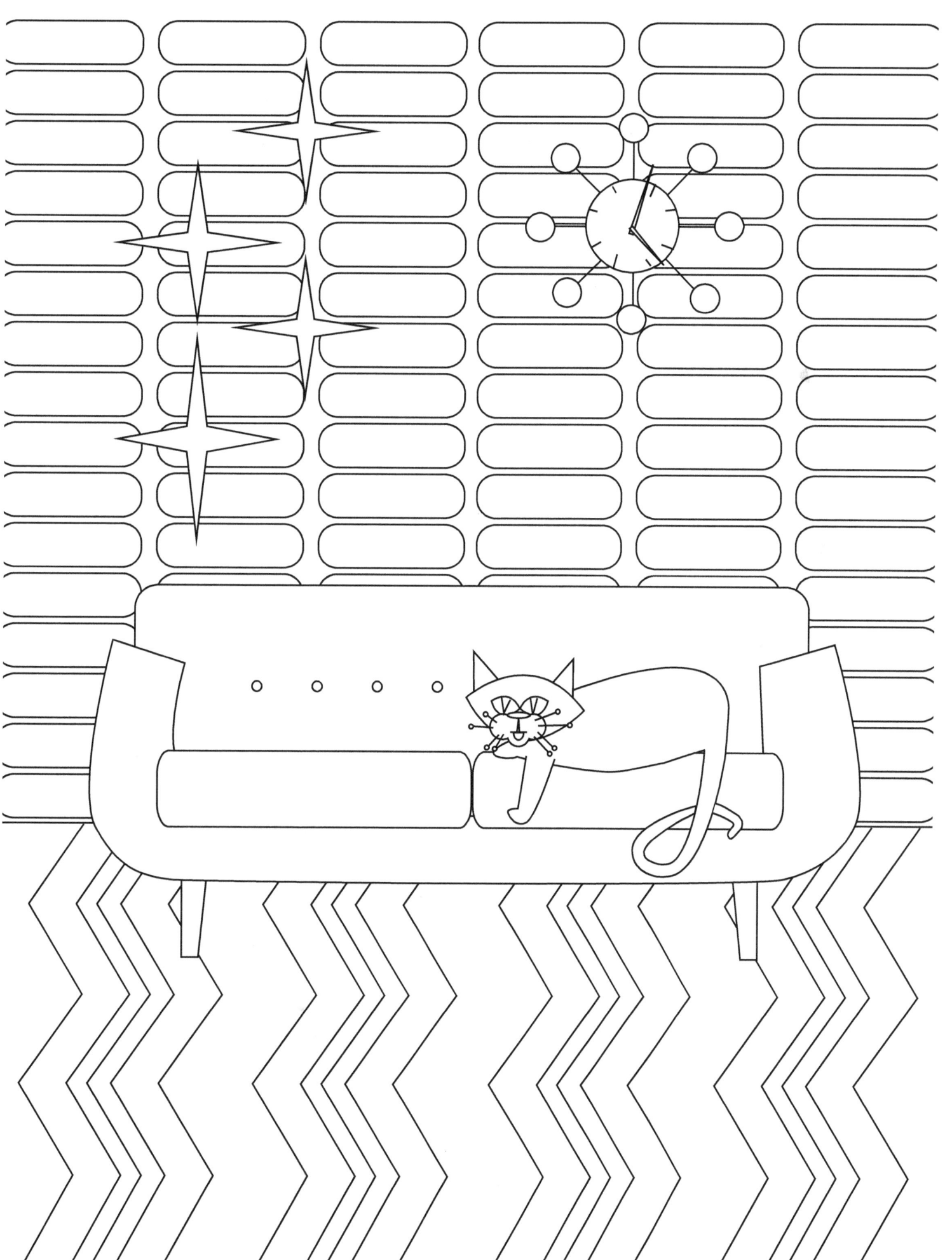

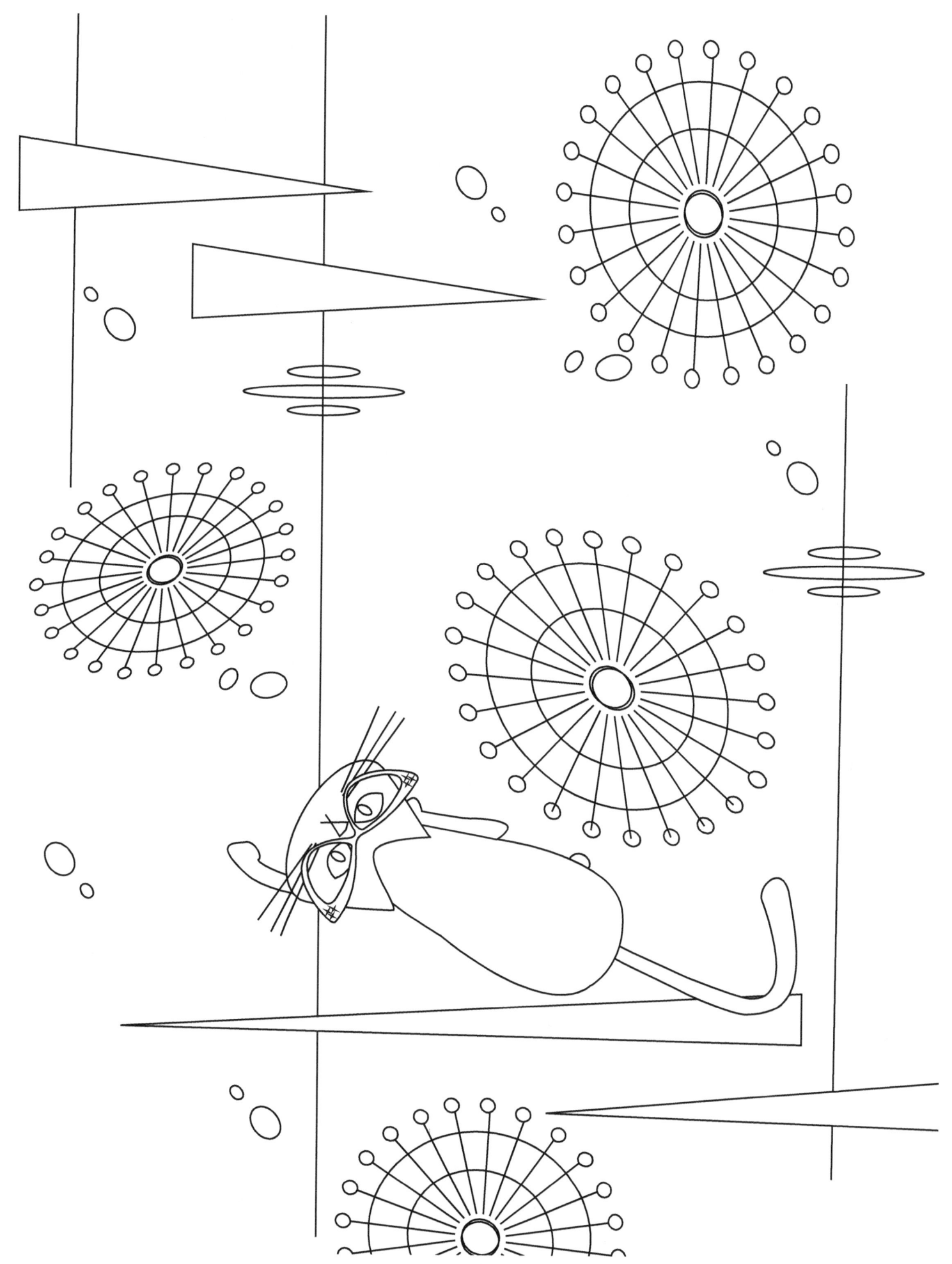

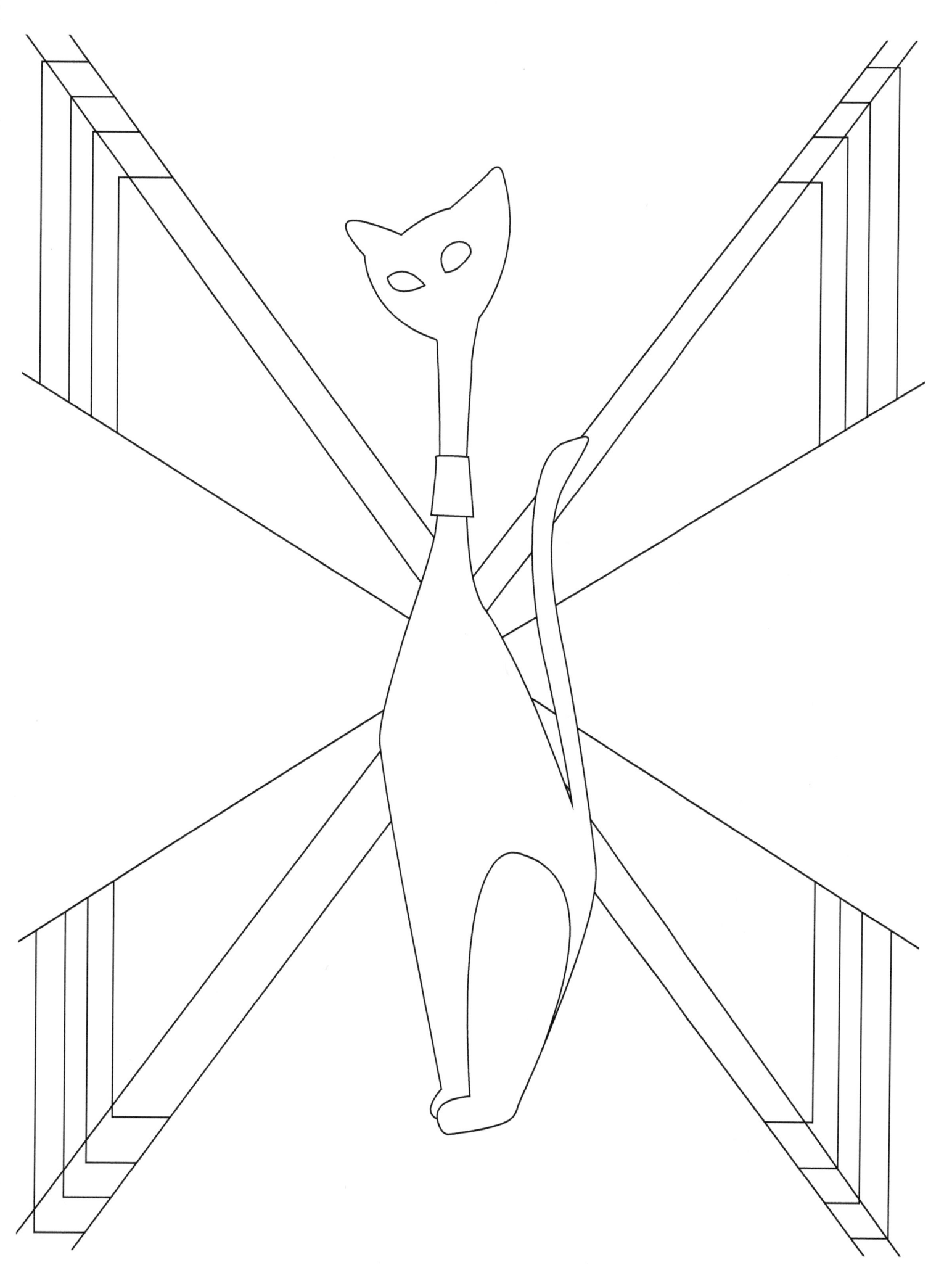

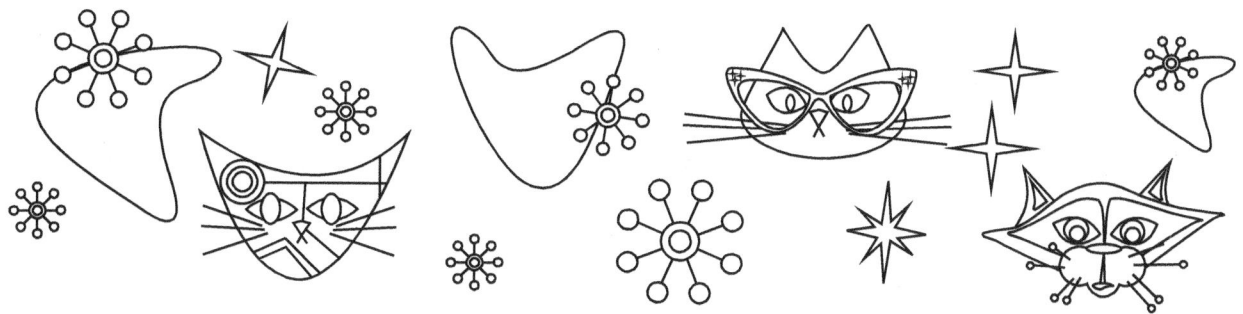

Thanks so much for choosing this coloring book, I hope you enjoyed it! Please connect with me on instagram and facebook with #retrocoloringbooks as I would love to get to share in the creativity you use to color these.

Look for future releases from me on my Amazon page by clicking follow on my author profile or by going to the website www.retrocoloringbooks.com

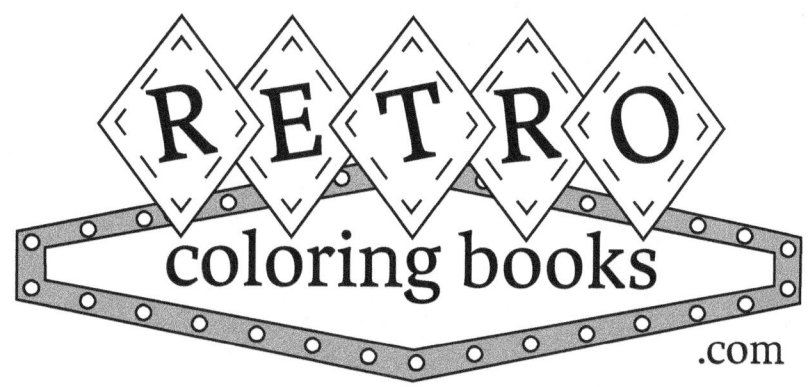

Retro Groovy Cats Coloring Book for Grown-ups, Volume 1
Copyright ©2016 Karen Douglas

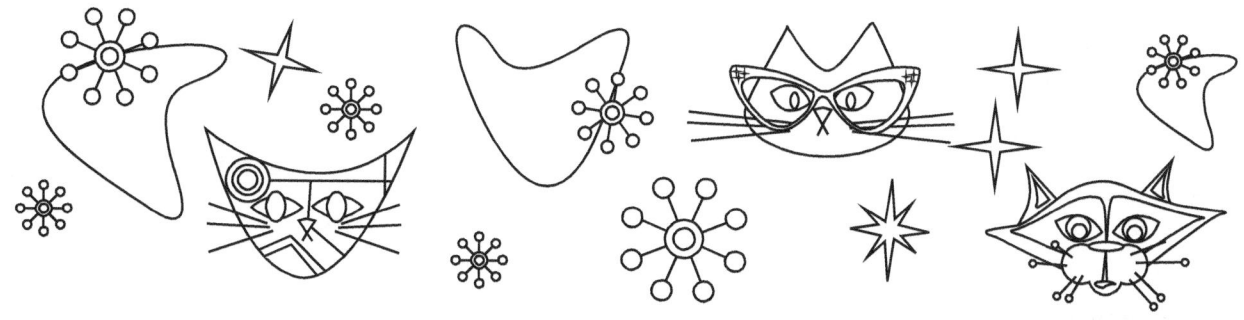